THE
VEGAN
SPIRALIZER
COOKBOOK

THE
VEGAN
SPIRALIZER
COOKBOOK

**Inspiring and Tasty Low Carb Spiralizer Recipes
for Everyone on a Vegan Diet – Use With Spiralizer,
Spiral Vegetable Cutter and Spaghetti Makers**

BETH SOLOMON

DISCLAIMER

The publisher and author make no representations or warranties with respect to the accuracy or completeness of the contents of this work and specially disclaim all warranties, including warranties without limitation warranties of fitness for a particular purpose. No warranties may be created or extended by sales or promotions. The information and strategies herein may not be suitable for every situation. This material is sold with the understanding that the author or publisher is not engaged in rendering medical, legal, or other professional advice or services. If professional help is required, the services of a competent professional should be sought. Neither the publisher nor the author shall be liable for damages arising here from. The fact that an individual or organisation is referred to in this work as a citation and/or possible source of further information or resource does not mean the author or the publisher endorses the information of the individual or organisation that they/it may provide or recommend.

Many of the designations used by manufacturers and sellers to distinguish their products are claimed as trademarks. Any and all product names referenced within this book are the trademarks of their respective owners. None of these owners have sponsored, endorsed or approved this book. Always read all information provided by the manufacturer's product labels or manuals before using their products. The author and publisher are not responsible for product claims made by manufacturers.

TRISTON PRESS

TABLE OF CONTENTS

①

BE VEGAN INSPIRED!

I was a really serious "food bum" for years. There was no way I would give up ham, dairy milk, eggs and cheese. No way! At least, so I thought. Then something really cool happened to me. I went to visit my sister in Ohio and I made friends with my sister's neighbor, Michael. He is a pretty big vegan fan and is absolutely crazy about eating well and being happy. Very influential indeed! Soon after I returned home, Michael sent me a spiralizer in the mail. I took my gift as a sign that I should start eating better. And so I did, then before I knew it, I got addicted to spiralizing. By the way, turning vegetables and fruits into noodles isn't just cute, but it's also fun! Gradually, I started adding more fruits and vegetables to my diet. It wasn't long before I decided to quit eating both meat and dairy and go vegan. I guess I was veganized. Yes, you read that right. I went vegan! For me, the spiralizer was an amazing gift. It has changed the way I usually think about vegetables. Thanks to Michael, my vegan friend. The benefits of eating vegan are superb. By using the spiralizer, the vegan lifestyle became even easier and more interesting.

After my obsession with vegan spiralizing grew, I began to experiment with different recipe ideas. My recipes quickly became a hit with family and friends. I also shared some of my recipes with Michael and even he was impressed. In fact, he later suggested that I should share some of my recipes with the vegan community.

Now, I must say that if you are looking for inspiring and tasty spiralizer recipes to support a vegan lifestyle, this cookbook is for you. Moreover, this cookbook will also be useful if you are looking for a healthy collection of delicious meat-free, egg-free and dairy-free spiralizer recipes.

Interestingly, with the vegan diet, we can all eat well and eat heartily without worry about weight gain. Additionally, with this cookbook, you'll be able to cook delicious vegan spiralizer meals for your breakfast, lunch and dinner menus. Whichever recipe you choose, you'll be indulging in an entirely healthy plant-based meal with easy-to-follow guidelines. Above all, I hope you enjoy these recipes as you embrace a healthy lifestyle. Welcome aboard vegans and everyone who wants to eat healthy spiralizer recipes. Let's start cooking some inspirational meals. Be vegan inspired!

VEGAN BREAKFAST RECIPES

Sweet Potato Pancakes

Start your morning with these hearty and delicious sweet potato pancakes. These nutrient-packed pancakes will be a delicious treat for the whole family.

MAKES: 4 servings
PREPARATION TIME: 10 minutes
COOKING TIME: 15 minutes

2 tablespoons Ground Flax Seeds
6 tablespoons Filtered Water
½ tablespoon Extra Virgin Olive Oil
2 medium Sweet Potatoes, peeled and spiralized
Sea Salt, to taste
Freshly Ground Black Pepper, to taste
3 tablespoons Pure Maple Syrup

Directions

1. In a bowl, mix together the flax seeds and water and set aside. In a large non-stick skillet, heat the oil on a medium heat. Add the sweet potato, salt and black pepper and cook, stirring occasionally, for 8 to10 minutes. Transfer the sweet potato into a large bowl and let it cool slightly before stirring in the flax seed mixture.
2. Meanwhile, preheat the griddle and grease it before cooking. In batches, pour the sweet potato mixture onto the preheated griddle and cook for 2 to 3 minutes. Carefully flip the pancake and cook for 1 to 2 minutes more.
3. Serve the pancakes with a topping of maple syrup.

Apple Pancakes

This is a delicious recipe which is perfect for a healthy breakfast. These moist pancakes are full of fantastic flavors and are very nutritious.

MAKES: 2 servings
PREPARATION TIME: 10 minutes
COOKING TIME: 5 minutes

¾ cup Whole Wheat Flour
¼ cup Oats
1 teaspoons Baking Powder
½ teaspoon Ground Cinnamon
⅛ teaspoon Ground Nutmeg
¼ teaspoon Sea Salt
1 cup Unsweetened Almond Milk
1 medium Apple, peeled and spiralized
¼ cup Raisins

Directions

1. Preheat the griddle and grease it before cooking.
2. In a large bowl, mix together the flour, oats, baking powder, cinnamon, nutmeg and salt. Add the milk and mix until combined before stirring in the apple and raisins.
3. In batches, pour the apple mixture onto the preheated griddle and cook for 2 to 3 minutes. Carefully flip the pancake and cook for a further 1 to 2 minutes before serving.

Buttered Sweet Potato Patties

This is an absolutely gorgeous and delicious sweet potato patty with peanut butter and fruits. This recipe may be a great hit for your kid's breakfast.

MAKES: 2 servings
PREPARATION TIME: 10 minutes (plus time to refrigerate)
COOKING TIME: 15 minutes

1 tablespoon Ground Flax Seeds
3 tablespoons Filtered Water
1½ tablespoons Extra Virgin Olive Oil
1 large Sweet Potato, peeled and spiralized
Sea Salt, to taste
Freshly Ground Black Pepper, to taste
¼ cup Peanut Butter
½ small Banana, peeled and mashed
4 Fresh Strawberries, hulled and sliced

Directions

1. In a bowl, mix together the flax seeds and water and set aside. In a large skillet, heat ½ tablespoon of the oil on a medium heat. Add the sweet potato and sprinkle with salt and black pepper. Cook for 6 to 8 minutes before transferring the sweet potato mixture into a bowl. Add the flax seed mixture and mix to combine. Transfer the mixture into 2 (6-ounce) ramekins, filling half full. Cover the ramekins with wax paper and place a weight over the paper to press firmly down. Refrigerate for at least 15 to

20 minutes.

2. In a large skillet, heat the remaining oil on a medium-low heat. Carefully transfer the sweet potato patties into the skillet. Cook for 3 to 4 minutes before turning and cooking for a further 2 to 3 minutes.

3. Meanwhile in a bowl, mix together the peanut butter and mashed banana. Place the patties onto serving plates. Evenly spread the peanut butter mixture over each patty. Top with strawberry slices and serve.

Mixed Vegetable Patties

This is a delicious combination of vegetables with a mild spicy touch. These savory patties, with a topping of almond butter will make a wonderful breakfast meal.

MAKES: 4 servings
PREPARATION TIME: 15 minutes
COOKING TIME: 6 minutes

2 tablespoons Ground Flax Seeds
6 tablespoons Filtered Water
1 small Zucchini, spiralized
1 small Yellow Squash, spiralized
1 small Carrot, peeled and spiralized
½ cup Chives, chopped
½ cup Almond Flour
1 teaspoon Ground Cumin
½ teaspoon Red Pepper Flakes, crushed
Sea Salt, to taste
Freshly Ground Black Pepper, to taste
2 tablespoons Extra Virgin Olive Oil
¼ cup Almond Butter
½ teaspoon Ground Cinnamon

Directions

1. In a bowl, mix together the flax seeds and water and set to one side. Mix together the remaining ingredients, except for the oil, butter and cinnamon, in another large bowl. Stir in flax seed mixture.
2. In a large skillet, heat ½ tablespoon of oil on a

medium-high heat. Place ¼ of the mixture in the oil and gently press down to form a patty. Cook for 5 to 6 minutes, turning once after 3 minutes. Repeat with the remaining oil and vegetable mixture.

3. Place the patties on serving plates. Spread the almond butter over each patty, sprinkle with the cinnamon and serve.

Sweet Potato Waffles

This is an absolutely delicious recipe for a fall morning or otherwise. These delicious sweet potato waffles, topped with maple syrup to make a festive breakfast.

MAKES: 2 servings
PREPARATION TIME: 10 minutes
COOKING TIME: 16 minutes

1 tablespoon Ground Flax Seeds
3 tablespoons Filtered Water
1 teaspoon Extra Virgin Olive Oil
1 medium Sweet Potato, peeled and spiralized
1 teaspoon Pumpkin Pie Spice
1 tablespoon Pure Maple Syrup

Directions

1. In a bowl, mix together the flax seeds and water and set aside. In a large non-stick skillet, heat the oil on a medium heat. Add the sweet potato and, while stirring occasionally, cook for about 10 minutes. Transfer the sweet potato into a large bowl and let it cool slightly. Add the pumpkin pie spice and mix well before stirring in the flax seed mixture.
2. Preheat the waffle iron and grease it before cooking. In batches, pour the sweet potato mixture into the preheated waffle iron. Cook for 5 to 6 minutes, or until golden brown.
3. Serve the waffles with a topping of maple syrup.

Potato & Herb Waffles

Here is a surprisingly delightful and exciting breakfast meal.
These waffles will be a great choice for a weekend breakfast.

MAKES: 2 servings
PREPARATION TIME: 10 minutes
COOKING TIME: 10 minutes

1 Russet Potato, peeled and spiralized
½ teaspoon Fresh Thyme, chopped
½ teaspoon Fresh Rosemary, chopped
Sea Salt, to taste
Freshly Ground Black Pepper, to taste

Directions

1. Preheat the waffle iron and grease it before cooking.
2. Squeeze the spiralized potato to remove any moisture. Transfer the squeezed potato into a large bowl and mix in the remaining ingredients. In batches, pour the sweet potato mixture into the preheated waffle iron. Cook for 8 to 10 minutes, or until golden brown.

Parsnip & Scallion Waffles

This is one of the perfect savory breakfasts for the cooler mornings. These warm and tasty waffles have a fluffy and slightly nutty texture.

MAKES: 4 servings
PREPARATION TIME: 10 minutes
COOKING TIME: 11 minutes

2 tablespoons Ground Flax Seeds
6 tablespoons Filtered Water
½ tablespoon Extra Virgin Olive Oil
1 Garlic Clove, minced
4 large Parsnips, peeled and spiralized
Sea Salt, to taste
Freshly Ground Black Pepper, to taste
¼ cup Scallions, finely chopped
2 tablespoons Pure Maple Syrup

Directions

1. Preheat the waffle iron and grease it before cooking.
2. In a bowl, mix together the flax seeds and water and set aside. In a large non-stick skillet, heat the oil on a medium heat. Sauté the garlic for 1 minute. Add the parsnip, black pepper and salt and, while stirring occasionally, cook for about 5 minutes. Transfer the parsnip mixture into a large bowl and let it cool slightly. Add the scallion and mix well before stirring in the flax seed mixture.
3. In batches, pour the parsnip mixture into the

preheated waffle iron. Cook for 4 to 5 minutes, or until golden brown. Serve the waffles with a topping of maple syrup.

Zucchini, Sweet Potato & Hash

This is a simple medley of zucchini and sweet potato in a satisfying hash brown breakfast dish. These hash browns are guaranteed to satisfy the whole family.

MAKES: 4 servings
PREPARATION TIME: 15 minutes (plus time to sit)
COOKING TIME: 12 minutes

2 small Zucchinis, spiralized and chopped
Sea Salt, to taste
1 medium Sweet Potato, peeled, spiralized and chopped
½ cup/1 whole White Onion, minced
Freshly Ground Black Pepper, to taste
1 tablespoon Coconut Oil, Organic and Extra Virgin

Directions

1. Place the zucchini and salt in a colander. Arrange the colander over a large bowl and set aside for 10 minutes before squeezing the extra moisture from the zucchini. Transfer the zucchini into a large bowl and mix in the sweet potato, onion, salt and black pepper.
2. In a large skillet, heat the oil on a medium heat. Form hash browns from the zucchini and sweet potato mixture and in batches, add the formed hash browns to the heated oil. Cook for 4 to 6 minutes. Carefully turn the hash browns and cook for a further 4 to 6 minutes.
3. Serve immediately.

Potato & Parsley Hash Browns

These delicious hash browns are crispy on the outside, firm and tasty inside. This is a great, versatile and easy recipe for breakfast.

MAKES: 2 servings
PREPARATION TIME: 15 minutes (plus time to sit)
COOKING TIME: 10 minutes

1 pound Red Potatoes, peeled and spiralized
Sea Salt, to taste
1 teaspoon Fresh Parsley, chopped
Freshly Ground Black Pepper, to taste
1 tablespoon Extra Virgin Olive Oil

Directions

1. Place the potatoes and salt in a colander. Arrange the colander over a large bowl and set aside for 10 minutes. Squeeze the extra moisture from the potatoes and transfer into a large bowl. Add the parsley, salt and black pepper and mix well.
2. In a large skillet, heat the oil on a medium heat. Form hash browns from the potato mixture and in batches; add the formed hash browns to the heated oil. Cook for 4 to 5 minutes. Carefully turn the hash browns and cook for a further 4 to 5 minutes.
3. Serve immediately.

Broccoli & Tofu Scramble

This is one of the healthiest and tastiest breakfast recipes for the whole family. Tofu adds a nutritious protein value to this dish.

MAKES: 2 servings
PREPARATION TIME: 15 minutes
COOKING TIME: 12 minutes

2 Broccoli Stems, spiralized
2 tablespoons Extra Virgin Olive Oil
½ Onion, chopped
1 small Red Bell Pepper, seeded and chopped
2 Garlic Cloves, minced
1 teaspoon Ground Turmeric
1 teaspoon Ground Cumin
1 (14-ounce) Block Extra Firm Tofu, crumbled and pressed
1 tablespoon Nutritional Yeast Flakes
Sea Salt, to taste
Freshly Ground Black Pepper, to taste

Directions

1. In a pan of boiling water, add the spiralized broccoli and cook for 2 to 3 minutes before removing from the heat and draining well.
2. In a large skillet, heat the oil on a medium heat. Sauté the onion and bell pepper for 4 to 5 minutes. Add the garlic, turmeric and cumin and sauté for 1 minute more. Add the remaining ingredients and cook for a further 2 to 3 minutes before serving hot.

Butternut Squash Skillet

This recipe makes a great tasting and filling breakfast meal. The spinach in this dish adds a healthy crunch, and the avocado brings a creamy texture to this skillet meal.

MAKES: 2 servings
PREPARATION TIME: 15 minutes
COOKING TIME: 35 minutes

¼ cup Whole Cherry Tomatoes
¼ cup Cherry Tomatoes, halved
2 tablespoons Extra Virgin Olive Oil
2 teaspoons Cayenne Pepper
Sea Salt, to taste
Freshly Ground Black Pepper, to taste
2 cups Butternut Squash, peeled and spiralized
1 Garlic Clove, minced
1 Jalapeño Pepper, seeded and chopped
3 cups Fresh Spinach, torn
1 small Avocado, peeled, pitted and cubed
¼ teaspoon Red Pepper Flakes, crushed
2 tablespoons minced Cilantro

Directions

1. Preheat the oven to 375 degrees F and line a baking dish with aluminum foil. In a bowl, mix together the tomatoes, 1 tablespoon of oil, cayenne pepper, salt and black pepper. Transfer the tomato mixture into the prepared baking dish and roast for about 25 minutes.

2. In a large skillet, heat the remaining oil on a medium heat. Add the spiralized squash and cook for 4 to 5 minutes. Transfer the squash in a large bowl. In the same skillet, add the garlic and jalapeño pepper and sauté for 1 minute. Add the spinach and avocado and cook for 2 minutes more. Stir in the cooked squash, roasted tomatoes and red pepper flakes. Cook for a further 2 minutes before garnishing with the cilantro and serving hot.

Sweet Potato with Quinoa

Here is a delicious and healthy bowl with beautiful colors and a sweet and savory texture. You will enjoy every bite of this healthy breakfast.

MAKES: 4 servings
PREPARATION TIME: 15 minutes
COOKING TIME: 20 minutes

For Dressing:
1 tablespoon Pure Maple Syrup
3 tablespoons Apple Cider Vinegar
1½ tablespoons Tahini
1 tablespoon Extra Virgin Olive Oil
1 tablespoon Filtered Water
Sea Salt, to taste
Freshly Ground Black Pepper, to taste

For Sweet Potato & Quinoa:
2 cups Filtered Water
¾ cup Uncooked Quinoa
1 tablespoon Extra Virgin Olive Oil
2 medium Sweet Potatoes, peeled and spiralized
½ teaspoon Garlic Powder
Sea Salt, to taste
Freshly Ground Black Pepper, to taste
2 tablespoons Raisins
2 tablespoons Almonds, toasted and chopped

Directions

1. For the dressing, mix together all of the dressing ingredients in a bowl before setting aside.
2. For the sweet potato and quinoa, add the water and quinoa to a pan and, over a medium heat, bring to a boil before reducing the heat and simmering for 15 to 20 minutes. Remove the pan from the heat and fluff with a fork. Meanwhile, in a skillet, heat the oil on a medium heat. Add the sweet potatoes, garlic powder, salt and black pepper. Cover and cook for 5 to 7 minutes. Uncover and cook, tossing once, for about 2 minutes.
3. Transfer the sweet potatoes into a large serving bowl. Stir in the quinoa and raisins. Drizzle with the dressing, top with the almonds and serve.

VEGAN LUNCH RECIPES

Chilled Cucumber & Mango Salad

This is a light and refreshing salad that is ideal for lunch time.
Enjoy this dish as a great choice for family or friends gatherings.

MAKES: 4 servings
PREPARATION TIME: 15 minutes (plus time to refrigerate)

For Dressing:
1 cup Fresh Mango, peeled, pitted and chopped
1 Jalapeño Pepper, seeded and minced
½ cup Soy-Free Veganaise
2 tablespoons Pure Maple Syrup
1 tablespoon Fresh Lime juice
Pinch of Sea Salt

For Salad:
2 large Cucumbers, spiralized
2 cups Fresh Mango, peeled, pitted and chopped

½ cup minced Cilantro Leaves
½ cup Cashew nuts, chopped

Directions

1. For the dressing, add all of the dressing ingredients into a blender and pulse until smooth.
2. For the salad, mix together the cucumber, mango and cilantro in a large bowl. Combine the dressing with the salad and toss to coat well. Refrigerate to chill before garnishing with the cashew nuts and serving.

Chilled Beet & Watermelon Soup

This is a delicious and hearty soup perfect for a lunchtime meal.
The spiralized beets give this soup an incredible heartiness.

MAKES: 4 servings
PREPARATION TIME: 15 minutes (plus time to refrigerate)

---

4 cups Fresh Watermelon, peeled, seeded, chopped and divided
1 small Cucumber, peeled, seeded and chopped
2 small Tomatoes, seeded and chopped
2 tablespoons Red Onion, chopped
¼ cup Fresh Cilantro Leaves
¼ cup Fresh Mint Leaves
2 tablespoons Fresh Lemon juice
1 tablespoon Balsamic Vinegar
1 tablespoon Extra Virgin Olive Oil
1 Jalapeño Pepper, seeded and minced
Sea Salt, to taste
Freshly Ground Black Pepper, to taste
2 medium Beets, peeled and spiralized

Directions

1. In a blender, add 3 cups of watermelon and the remaining ingredients, except for the beets, and pulse until smooth. Transfer the soup into a large bowl. Cover and refrigerate to chill for at least 2 to 3 hours.
2. Before serving, top with the remaining watermelon

and the spiralized beets.

Chilled Zucchini & Squash Soup

This delicious soup makes a perfect lunchtime dish for the whole family. It may quickly become a lunchtime favorite.

MAKES: 4 servings
PREPARATION TIME: 15 minutes (plus time to refrigerate)
COOKING TIME: 30 minutes

2 tablespoons Extra Virgin Olive Oil
1 small Yellow Onion, chopped
2 small Garlic Cloves, minced
1 teaspoon Dried Oregano, crushed
¼ teaspoon Red Pepper Flakes, crushed
1 large Yellow Squash, chopped
Sea Salt, to taste
Freshly Ground Black Pepper, to taste
⅔ cup Homemade Vegetable Broth
1½ cups Filtered Water
1 tablespoon Fresh Lemon juice
1 small Zucchini, spiralized
¼ cup Basil Leaves, freshly chopped

Directions:

1. In a large soup pan, heat the oil on a medium heat. Sauté the onion for 8 to 9 minutes before adding the garlic, oregano and red pepper flakes and sautéing for 1 minute more. Add the chopped yellow squash, salt and black pepper and cook, whilst stirring occasionally, for 8 to 10 minutes. Add the broth and water and bring to a boil on a high heat before reducing the heat and simmering for about 10

minutes. Remove the soup pan from the heat and let it cool slightly.

2. In a blender, add the soup and lemon juice and pulse in batches until smooth. Transfer the soup into a large bowl and season with salt and black pepper. Cover the soup and refrigerate to chill. Top with the spiralized zucchini and basil and serve.

Spicy Sweet Potato Soup

This is a deliciously spicy soup with sweet potato noodles and a luxurious bite of avocado. The softness of the spiralized sweet potato adds a delicious perfection to this dish.

MAKES: 2 servings
PREPARATION TIME: 15 minutes
COOKING TIME: 15 minutes

1 tablespoon Extra Virgin Olive Oil
1 White Onion, chopped
1 Garlic Clove, minced
1 Serrano Peeper, seeded and chopped
½ teaspoon Ground Cumin
½ tablespoon Cayenne Pepper
2 cups Fresh Tomatoes, finely chopped
3 cups Homemade Vegetable Broth
1 large Sweet Potato, peeled and spiralized
Sea Salt, to taste
Freshly Ground Black Pepper, to taste
1 medium Avocado, peeled, pitted and cubed
2 tablespoons Parsley Leaves, freshly chopped

Directions

1. In a large soup pan, heat the oil on a medium heat. Sauté the onion for 3 to 4 minutes before adding the garlic, Serrano pepper, cumin and cayenne and sautéing for 1 minute more. Add the tomatoes and cook, crushing occasionally, for 2 to 3 minutes. Add the broth and bring to a boil before stirring in the

sweet potato. Reduce the heat to medium-low, cover, and simmer for 6 to 7 minutes.

2. Stir in the salt, black pepper and avocado and immediately remove the pan from the heat. Garnish with the parsley and serve hot.

Vegetable Wraps

These salad wraps are filled with fresh vegetables, black beans and a delicious sauce. These wraps are guaranteed to be a hit as a light lunch.

MAKES: 4 servings
PREPARATION TIME: 20 minutes

For Sauce:
2 cups Fresh Spinach Leaves
½ cup Fresh Cilantro Leaves
2 large Garlic Cloves chopped
⅓ cup Cashew nuts
½ cup Extra Virgin Olive Oil
Sea Salt, to taste
Freshly Ground Black Pepper, to taste

For Wraps:
1 medium Cucumber, spiralized and chopped
1 small Carrot, peeled, spiralized and chopped
1 large Orange Bell Pepper, seeded and thinly sliced
½ medium Avocado, peeled, pitted and thinly sliced
4 large Lettuce Leaves, trimmed

Directions

1. For the sauce, add all of the sauce ingredients into a blender and pulse until smooth. Transfer the sauce into a bowl and refrigerate before serving.
2. For the wraps, mix together the cucumber, carrot, bell pepper and avocado in a bowl. Place a lettuce

leaf on a large plate and arrange ¼ of the vegetable mixture over the leaf. Top with ¼ of the sauce before rolling the leaves around the vegetable mixture. Repeat with the remaining leaves, vegetable mixture and sauce before serving immediately.

Roasted Sweet Potato Wraps

These savory wraps, filled with the goodness of roasted sweet potatoes, make a wonderfully delicious and a light meal.

MAKES: 4 servings
PREPARATION TIME: 20 minutes
COOKING TIME: 30 minutes

For Sweet Potato:
2 Sweet Potatoes, peeled and spiralized
1 tablespoon Extra Virgin Olive Oil
¼ teaspoon Red Pepper Flakes, crushed
Sea Salt, to taste
Freshly Ground Black Pepper, to taste

For Wraps:
4 large Romaine Lettuce Leaves
½ cup Soy-Free Veganaise
⅛ teaspoon Red Pepper Flakes, crushed
1 medium Carrot, peeled and spiralized

Directions:

1. Preheat the oven to 375 degrees F and line a large baking sheet with foil paper before placing the sweet potato into prepared baking sheet. Drizzle the sweet potato with the oil and season with the remaining sweet potato ingredients. Roast for about 30 minutes before removing them from the oven and letting them cool.

2. Place the lettuce leaves on large plates. Evenly spread the veganaise over each leaf and sprinkle with the red pepper flakes. Top with the roasted

sweet potato and carrot. Roll the leaves around vegetable mixture and serve immediately.

Zucchini & Bean Tortillas

This recipe makes a whole grain tortilla vegetable wrap that is really quick, delicious and fresh. These tortillas are a real feast for the whole family.

MAKES: 2 servings
PREPARATION TIME: 15 minutes

For Sauce:
½ cup cooked Chickpeas, drained
1 tablespoon Tahini
1 small Garlic Clove, chopped
½ tablespoon Extra Virgin Olive Oil
½ tablespoon Fresh Lemon juice
Sea Salt, to taste
Freshly Ground Black Pepper, to taste

For Tortillas:
1 small Carrot, peeled, spiralized and chopped
1 small Zucchini, spiralized and chopped
¼ cup cooked Black Beans, drained
Sea Salt, to taste
Freshly Ground Black Pepper, to taste
2 (8-inch) Whole Grain Tortillas

Directions:
1. For the sauce, add all of the sauce ingredients into a blender and pulse until smooth.
2. In a large bowl, mix together all of the tortilla ingredients, except for the tortillas. Place a tortilla

on a large plate and spread half of the sauce over the tortilla. Top with half of the vegetable mixture and roll the tortilla. Repeat with the remaining tortilla and serve immediately.

Creamy Zucchini Rolls

These tasty vegetarian rolls are beautifully dressed with zucchini and spinach, topped with a delicious creamy sauce.

MAKES: 2 servings
PREPARATION TIME: 15 minutes

For Sauce:
1 small Garlic Clove, minced
½ Serrano Pepper, seeded and minced
¼ cup Peanut Butter
1 tablespoon Coconut Aminos
½ tablespoon Rice Vinegar
½ tablespoon Sesame Oil
Pinch of Red Pepper Flakes, crushed
½ cup Warm Water

For Wraps:
2 small Zucchinis, spiralized
¼ cup Red Onion, chopped
2 cups Spinach Leaves, freshly chopped
2 Whole Wheat Sandwich Wraps

Directions

1. For the sauce, mix together all of the sauce ingredients in a bowl. In another large bowl, mix together all of the wrap ingredients, except for the wraps. Drizzle the sauce over the vegetables and gently toss to coat well.
2. Place a wrap on a large plate and top with half of the

vegetable mixture before rolling the wrap. Repeat with the remaining wrap before serving immediately.

Fresh Vegetable Bowl

This is a quick and healthy lunch recipe that tastes like fresh spring rolls. This creamy vegetable bowl is fantastically delicious.

MAKES: 2 servings
PREPARATION TIME: 15 minutes

For Sauce:
2 tablespoons peeled Avocado, pitted and mashed
2 tablespoons Peanut Butter
1 tablespoon Coconut Aminos
½ teaspoon Rice Vinegar
½ tablespoon Pure Maple Syrup
½ tablespoon Filtered Water
Pinch of Red Pepper Flakes, crushed

For Vegetable Bowl:
⅔ cup Unsweetened Coconut Milk
2 small Zucchinis, spiralized
2 cups Cabbage, spiralized
1 small Carrot, peeled and spiralized
2 tablespoons Mint Leaves, freshly chopped
2 tablespoons Peanuts, toasted

Directions:
1. For the sauce, beat together all of the sauce ingredients in a bowl.
2. Divide the coconut milk into 4 serving bowls. Add the vegetables and mint and gently mix before

topping with the sauce. Garnish with the peanuts and serve immediately.

Roasted Beet & Cherry Tomatoes

The simple and tasty flavors of roasted beets and cherry tomatoes complement each other nicely. This recipe makes a simple and easy lunchtime meal.

MAKES: 2 servings
PREPARATION TIME: 15 minutes
COOKING TIME: 25 minutes

10-12 Fresh Cherry Tomatoes
3 teaspoons Extra Virgin Olive Oil
½ teaspoon Garlic Powder
Sea Salt, to taste
Freshly Ground Black Pepper, to taste
2 large Beets, trimmed, peeled and spiralized
2 tablespoons minced Cilantro Leaves

Directions:

1. Preheat the oven to 400 degrees F. Arrange the tomatoes on a baking dish and drizzle with half of the oil. Sprinkle with the garlic powder, salt and black pepper and roast for about 15 minutes. Remove the baking dish from the oven.
2. Place the beets into the baking dish and drizzle with the remaining oil. Sprinkle with the garlic powder, salt and black pepper and roast for a further 10 minutes. Garnish with the cilantro before serving.

VEGAN DINNER RECIPES

Beets & Olives with Quinoa

This is a filling and lively meal for the whole family. Enjoy this quinoa dish with beet noodles, olives and baby greens that has a great texture with beautiful colors and flavors combined.

MAKES: 2 servings
PREPARATION TIME: 15 minutes
COOKING TIME: 15 minutes

½ cup Homemade Vegetable Broth
¼ cup Quinoa, rinsed
1 large Beet trimmed, peeled and spiralized
¼ cup Black Olives pitted and sliced
¼ cup Green Olives pitted and sliced
2 cups Fresh Baby Greens
2 tablespoons Extra Virgin Olive Oil
2 tablespoons Fresh Lime juice
Sea Salt, to taste
Freshly Ground Black Pepper, to taste

¼ cup Walnuts, toasted and chopped

Directions:

1. In a pan, add the broth and quinoa and bring to a boil on a medium-high heat. Once boiling, lower the heat and simmer for about 15 minutes, covered. Turn off the heat and let the pan stand for 5 minutes, covered. With a fork, fluff the quinoa.
2. Meanwhile, in a large bowl mix together the remaining ingredients, except for the walnuts. Add the cooked quinoa and toss to coat well. Top with the walnuts and serve.

Zucchini & Mushroom Soup

*This dish is an amazingly delicious, healthy and easy
vegetable soup that has a combination of zucchini,
mushrooms and spinach.*

MAKES: 2 servings
PREPARATION TIME: 15 minutes
COOKING TIME: 15 minutes

*1 tablespoon Extra Virgin Olive Oil
1 small White Onion, chopped
1 Celery Stalk, chopped
2 Garlic Cloves, minced
¼ teaspoon Dried Thyme, crushed
¼ teaspoon Red Pepper Flakes, crushed
1 cup Button Mushrooms, chopped
2 cups Fresh Kale, trimmed and chopped
2½ cups Homemade Vegetable Broth
2 tablespoons Coconut Aminos
1 large Zucchini, spiralized
½ cup Scallion, chopped
Sea Salt, to taste
Freshly Ground Black Pepper, to taste
1 large Avocado, peeled, pitted and cubed*

Directions:

1. In a large soup pan, heat the oil on a medium heat.
Add the onion and celery and sauté for 3 to 4
minutes. Add the garlic, thyme and red pepper
flakes and sauté for 1 minute. Add the mushrooms

and kale and cook for about 2 minutes more. Add the broth and bring to a boil. Stir in coconut aminos, reduce the heat to low and simmer for about 5 minutes.

2. Stir in the zucchini and scallions and cook for a further 2 to 3 minutes. Season with salt and black pepper and remove from the heat. Garnish with the avocado and serve hot.

Zucchini & Tofu Soup

This is a healthy and flavorful zucchini noodle and tofu soup ideal for a dinner. The use of curry powder provides a subtle yet wonderful taste to the zucchini and tofu.

MAKES: 2 servings
PREPARATION TIME: 15 minutes
COOKING TIME: 8 minutes

1 teaspoon Sesame Oil
½ teaspoon Fresh Ginger, minced
1 tablespoon Curry Powder
½ cup Tofu, cubed
3 cups Homemade Vegetable Broth
1 teaspoon Coconut Aminos
2 medium Zucchinis, spiralized
½ cup Scallions, chopped
Sea Salt, to taste
Freshly Ground Black Pepper, to taste
¼ cup Fresh Basil, chopped

Directions:

1. In a large soup pan, heat the oil on a medium heat. Add the ginger and curry powder and sauté for about 1 minute. Add the tofu and broth and bring to a boil. Stir in the coconut aminos, reduce the heat to low and simmer for 3 to 4 minutes.
2. Stir in the zucchini and scallions and cook for a further 2 to 3 minutes. Season with salt and black pepper and remove from the heat. Garnish with

basil and serve hot.

Carrot & Corn Soup

This flavorsome, healthy and sophisticated soup is perfect for the whole family.

MAKES: 4 servings
PREPARATION TIME: 15 minutes
COOKING TIME: 20 minutes

2 tablespoons Extra Virgin Olive Oil
1 small Yellow Onion, chopped
2 Celery Stalks, chopped
2 Garlic Cloves, minced
½ teaspoon Dried Oregano, crushed
½ teaspoon Dried Thyme, crushed
½ teaspoon Red Pepper Flakes, crushed
4½ cups Homemade Vegetable Broth
2 cups Fresh Corn
1 large Carrot, peeled and spiralized
Sea Salt, to taste
Freshly Ground Black Pepper, to taste
½ cup Basil Leaves, freshly chopped

Directions:

1. In a large soup pan, heat the oil on a medium heat. Add the onion and celery and sauté for 3 to 4 minutes. Add the garlic, dried herbs and red pepper flakes and sauté for about 1 minute. Add the broth and corn and bring to a boil before reducing the heat and simmering for 8 to 10 minutes.
2. Stir in carrot and cook for about 4 to 5 minutes.

Season with salt and black pepper and remove from the heat. Garnish with basil and serve hot.

Sweet Potato & Vegetable Stew

This recipe makes a hearty, filling and delicious stew that is perfect for a cold winter night. This dish is also packed with healthy nutrients from the vegetables.

MAKES: 4 servings
PREPARATION TIME: 20 minutes
COOKING TIME: 45 minutes

1 tablespoon Extra Virgin Olive Oil
1 medium White Onion, chopped
2 Celery Stalks, chopped
1 large Carrot, peeled and chopped
3-4 Garlic Cloves, minced
1 Bay Leaf
½ teaspoon Dried Oregano, crushed
½ teaspoon Dried Thyme, crushed
½ teaspoon Red Pepper Flakes, crushed
2 cups Fresh Tomatoes, finely chopped
1½ cups cooked Navy Beans
3 cups Homemade Vegetable Broth
1 large Sweet Potato, peeled and spiralized
3 cups Fresh Spinach, torn
3 tablespoons Fresh Lemon juice
Sea Salt, to taste
Freshly Ground Black Pepper, to taste
½ cup Fresh Cilantro, chopped

Directions:

1. In a large soup pan, heat the oil on a medium heat.

Add the onion, celery and carrot and sauté for 6 to 7 minutes. Add the garlic, bay leaf, dried herbs and red pepper flakes and sauté for 1 minute more. Add the tomatoes and cook, whilst crushing, for 1 to 2 minutes. Add the beans and broth and bring to a boil before reducing the heat and simmering, whilst stirring occasionally, for about 25 minutes.

2. Stir in the sweet potato and spinach and simmer for a further 10 minutes. Stir in the lemon juice, salt, black pepper and cilantro and remove from heat before serve hot.

Zucchini & Chickpeas Stew

Enjoy this flavorful stew which will be a great hit for a warm and cozy night. Surely this stew is a good way to get your daily intake of healthy vegetables.

YIELD: 4 servings
PREPARATION TIME: 20 minutes
COOKING TIME: 45 minutes

2 tablespoons Extra Virgin Olive Oil
1 Medium Yellow Onion, chopped
1 Celery Stalk, chopped
2 Red Bell Pepper, seeded and chopped
1 Large Carrot, peeled and chopped
3-4 Garlic Cloves, minced
1 teaspoon Fresh Ginger, minced
1 Serrano Pepper, chopped
½ teaspoon Cayenne Pepper
2 cups Fresh Tomatoes, finely chopped finely
2 cups Cooked Chickpeas
3 cups Homemade Vegetable Broth
1 Large Zucchini, spiralized
Sea Salt, to taste
Freshly Ground Black Pepper, to taste
¼ cup Basil Leaves, freshly chopped

Directions:

1. In a large pan, heat the oil on a medium heat. Add the onion, celery, bell pepper and carrot and sauté

for 8 to 10 minutes. Add the garlic, ginger, Serrano pepper and cayenne pepper and sauté for about 1 minute. Add the tomatoes and cook, crushing, for 3 to 4 minutes.

2. Add the chickpeas and broth and bring to a boil before reducing the heat and simmering, covered, for 20 to 25 minutes. Stir in the zucchini and simmer for a further 5 minutes. Season with salt and black pepper and remove from the heat. Top with basil and serve hot.

Sweet Potato with Chickpeas

This is a wonderfully delicious and healthy meal for the whole family. The creamy sauce in this dish adds a nice flavor to the combo of sweet potato and chickpeas.

YIELD: 4 servings
PREPARATION TIME: 15 minutes
COOKING TIME: 35 minutes

For Chickpeas:
2 cups Cooked Chickpeas
1 teaspoon Extra Virgin Olive Oil
1 teaspoon Cayenne Pepper
½ teaspoon Ground Cumin
¼ teaspoon Red Pepper Flakes, crushed

For Sweet Potato:
1 tablespoon Extra Virgin Olive Oil
1 Garlic Clove, minced
1 Large Sweet Potato, peeled and spiralized
Sea Salt and Freshly Ground Black Pepper, to taste
3 cups Swiss Chard, chopped

For Sauce:
¼ cup Unsweetened Almond Milk
¼ cup Raw Cashews, soaked for 2 hours and drained
2 Garlic Cloves, chopped
½ teaspoon Dijon Mustard
½ tablespoon Fresh Lemon Juice
Sea Salt and Freshly Ground Black Pepper, to taste

Directions:

1. Preheat the oven to 400 degrees F. Line a baking sheet with parchment paper. For chickpeas in a bowl, add all ingredients and toss to coat well. Roast for about 30 to 35 minutes, tossing once after 18 minutes.

2. Meanwhile in a large skillet, heat oil on medium heat. Add garlic and sauté for about 1 minute. Add sweet potato and cook for about 5 to 6 minutes. Stir in Swiss chard and cook for 3 to 4 minutes. Transfer the mixture into a large serving bowl.

3. For the sauce, add all of the ingredients into a blender and pulse until smooth. Pour the sauce over the sweet potato mixture and gently toss to coat. Top with the roasted chickpeas and serve warm.

Roasted Zucchini & Sweet Potato

This is a recipe for an easy and quick meal for the whole family. The roasted sweet potato and zucchini makes for a wonderfully flavorful combination.

MAKES: 2 servings
PREPARATION TIME: 15 minutes
COOKING TIME: 20 minutes

1 medium Sweet Potato, peeled and spiralized
2 large Zucchinis, spiralized
1 tablespoon Extra Virgin Olive Oil
1 teaspoon Dried Rosemary, crushed
½ teaspoon Garlic Powder
½ teaspoon Red Pepper Flakes, crushed
½ teaspoon Ground Cumin
Sea Salt, to taste
Freshly Ground Black Pepper, to taste
2 tablespoons Walnuts, toasted and chopped

Directions:

1. Preheat the oven to 400 degrees F and line a large baking sheet with parchment paper.
2. In a large bowl, add all of the ingredients and toss to coat well. Transfer the mixture into the prepared baking sheet and roast for about 20 minutes. Garnish with the walnuts and serve.

Zucchini with Asparagus

This recipe makes a luxurious and surprisingly delicious dish for dinner. This meal is a great combination of soft zucchini noodles, onion, tasty asparagus and crunchy almonds.

MAKES: 2 servings
PREPARATION TIME: 15 minutes
COOKING TIME: 25 minutes

¼ cup Balsamic Vinegar
8 White Pearl Onions, peeled
6-8 Asparagus Stalks, trimmed and cut into 2-inch pieces
2 tablespoons Extra Virgin Olive Oil
1 teaspoon Dried Rosemary, crushed
½ teaspoon Red Pepper Flakes, crushed
Sea Salt, to taste
Freshly Ground Black Pepper, to taste
2 Garlic Cloves, minced
1 Jalapeño Pepper, seeded and chopped
2 medium Zucchinis, spiralized
2 tablespoons Almonds, toasted and chopped
2 tablespoons minced Cilantro Leaves

Directions

1. Preheat the oven to 375 degrees F. In a bowl, mix together the vinegar and onion. Arrange the asparagus in a large baking dish and drizzle with 1 tablespoon of oil. Place the onion into the baking dish with the asparagus and sprinkle with the rosemary, red pepper flakes, salt and black pepper.

Roast for about 25 minutes, tossing once after 13 minutes.

2. Meanwhile, heat the remaining oil on a medium heat in a large skillet. Add the garlic and jalapeño pepper and sauté for about 1 minute. Add the zucchini and cook for about 2 to 3 minutes. Transfer the zucchini into a serving bowl and top with the asparagus mixture. Garnish with the cilantro and almonds before serving.

Sautéed Zucchini & Mushrooms

This is one of the easiest and tastiest vegetable meals to make. The spiralized zucchini combines nicely with the shiitake mushroom in this dish.

MAKES: 2 servings
PREPARATION TIME: 15 minutes
COOKING TIME: 15 minutes

1½ tablespoons Extra Virgin Olive Oil
½ small Onion, chopped
1 Garlic Clove, minced
½ teaspoon Red Pepper Flakes, crushed
1 large Tomato, finely chopped
2 cups Shiitake Mushrooms, chopped
2 medium Zucchinis, spiralized
1 tablespoon Fresh Lime juice
Sea Salt, to taste
Freshly Ground Black Pepper, to taste
1 teaspoon Lime Zest, freshly grated
2 tablespoons Basil Leaves, freshly chopped

Directions:

1. In a large skillet, heat the oil on a medium heat. Sauté the onion for 4 to 5 minutes before adding the garlic and red pepper flakes and sautéing for about 1 minute. Add the chopped tomato and cook, whilst stirring occasionally, for 2 to 3 minutes. Add the Mushrooms and cook for about 2 to 3 minutes.
2. Add zucchini and cook for about 2 to 3 minutes. Stir

in lime juice, salt and black pepper and remove from heat. Garnish with lime zest and basil and serve.

Zucchini with Creamy Sauce

Here is a great example of healthy eating with nice flavors! This creamy cauliflower sauce brings a flavorful richness to the sautéed zucchini.

MAKES: 4 servings
PREPARATION TIME: 15 minutes
COOKING TIME: 12 minutes

For Sauce:
4 cups Cauliflower Florets
2 Garlic Cloves, chopped
2 tablespoons Flax Seeds
½ tablespoon Extra Virgin Olive Oil
½ cup Unsweetened Almond Milk
1 tablespoon Fresh Lemon juice
1 teaspoon Dried Oregano, crushed
1 teaspoon Dried Thyme, crushed
Sea Salt, to taste
Freshly Ground Black Pepper, to taste

For Zucchini:
2 tablespoons Extra Virgin Olive Oil
4 large Zucchinis, spiralized
4 cups Fresh Kale, trimmed and chopped
¼ cup Basil Leaves, freshly chopped

Directions:
1. In a large pan of boiling water, add the cauliflower and cook for 5 to 6 minutes. Remove from the heat

and drain well before setting aside to cool. In a blender, add the cauliflower and remaining sauce ingredients, and pulse until smooth and creamy.

2. In a large skillet, heat the oil on a medium heat. Add the zucchini and kale and sauté for 3 to 4 minutes. Stir in the sauce and cook for 1 to 2 minutes, or until heated through. Garnish with the basil and serve hot.

Sautéed Lemony Broccoli

This is a super quick and flavorful broccoli dish. The fresh lemon juice and zest adds a wonderfully refreshing touch to this dish.

MAKES: 2 servings
PREPARATION TIME: 15 minutes
COOKING TIME: 12 minutes

2 tablespoons Extra Virgin Olive Oil
2 Garlic Cloves, minced
¼ teaspoon Red Pepper Flakes, crushed
1 large Broccoli Head, cut into florets
1 large Broccoli Stem, spiralized
1 tablespoon Fresh Lemon juice
Sea Salt, to taste
Freshly Ground Black Pepper, to taste
2 tablespoons Pecans, toasted and chopped
½ teaspoon Lemon Zest, freshly grated

Directions:

1. In a large skillet, heat the oil on a medium heat. Sauté the red pepper flakes and garlic for about 1 minute. Add the broccoli florets and noodles and cook for a further 8 to 10 minutes. Stir in the lemon juice, salt and black pepper and remove from the heat.
2. Garnish with the lemon zest and pecans before serving.

Butternut Squash with Lentils

This is one of the most delicious vegan dinner meals. Enjoy this thick textured dish that is packed with a healthy source of protein.

MAKES: 4 servings
PREPARATION TIME: 15 minutes
COOKING TIME: 52 minutes

1 cup Filtered Water
½ cup Red Lentils, rinsed
1 tablespoon Extra Virgin Olive Oil
½ Red Onion, chopped
1 cup Scallions, chopped
1 Celery Stalk, chopped
2 Garlic Cloves, minced
1 Jalapeño Pepper, seeded and chopped
½ tablespoon Fresh Thyme, chopped
1 medium Butternut Squash, peeled, spiralized and chopped
Sea Salt, to taste
Freshly Ground Black Pepper, to taste
½ cup Raisins
½ cup Walnuts, chopped
2 tablespoons Fresh Cilantro, chopped

Directions:

1. In a pan, add the water and lentils and bring to a boil on a medium-high heat before reducing the heat and simmering until the lentils are cooked, for 30 to 35 minutes.
2. In a large skillet, heat the oil on a medium heat. Add

the onion, scallion and celery and sauté for 3 to 4 minutes. Add the garlic, jalapeño pepper and thyme and sauté for 1 minute more. Stir in the squash, salt and black pepper and cook, whilst stirring occasionally, for 8 to 10 minutes. Stir in the cooked lentils, raisins and walnuts and cook for 1 to 2 minutes more. Garnish with the cilantro and serve immediately.

VEGAN SALAD RECIPES

Apple, Pear & Mixed Fruit Salad

This is a fun to eat mixed fruit salad with a sweet and slightly tangy strawberry dressing. This fresh fruit salad is so inviting and full of vibrant colors, everyone will love it.

MAKES: 4 servings
PREPARATION TIME: 20 minutes

For Dressing:
½ cup Fresh Strawberries, hulled and sliced
1 tablespoon Pure Maple Syrup
2 tablespoons Fresh Lemon juice

For Salad:
1 Apple, peeled and spiralized
1 Pear, peeled and spiralized or julienned
1 cup Melon, peeled, seeded and cubed
1 cup Watermelon, peeled, seeded and cubed
1 cup Fresh Strawberries, hulled and sliced

1 cup Fresh Blackberries
1 cup Fresh Blueberries

Directions:

1. For the dressing, add all of the dressing ingredients into a blender and pulse until smooth.
2. Mix together all of the fruits in a large serving bowl. Mix the dressing with the salad, toss to coat well and serve immediately.

Apple & Spinach Salad

This is one of the easiest and healthiest salads you will make. The sweet and sour mustard dressing gives a really delicious touch to the apple and spinach, while the walnuts provide a wonderfully nutty texture.

MAKES: 2 servings
PREPARATION TIME: 10 minutes

For Dressing:
2 tablespoons Extra Virgin Olive Oil
2 tablespoons Apple Cider Vinegar
1 tablespoon Pure Maple Syrup
1 teaspoon Fresh Lemon juice
1 tablespoon Dijon Mustard
Sea Salt, to taste
Freshly Ground Black Pepper, to taste

For Salad:
2 large Apples, peeled and spiralized
4 cups Fresh Baby Spinach
½ cup Walnuts, toasted and chopped

Directions:
1. Beat together all of the dressing ingredients in a bowl.
2. In another large serving bowl, mix together the apple and spinach. Combine the dressing with the salad, tossing to coat well. Garnish with the walnuts

and serve immediately.

Apple, Pear & Greens Salad

This recipe has a wonderful combination of ingredients. The tanginess of the dressing and the crunchiness of the almonds complement each other nicely, especially with the freshness of the fruit and baby greens.

MAKES: 2 servings
PREPARATION TIME: 15 minutes

For Dressing:
2 tablespoons Extra Virgin Olive Oil
2 tablespoons Apple Cider Vinegar
1 tablespoon Pure Maple Syrup
1 tablespoon Dijon Mustard
Sea Salt, to taste
Freshly Ground Black Pepper, to taste

For Salad:
1 large Apple, peeled and spiralized
1 large Pear, peeled and spiralized or julienned
¼ cup Fresh Cranberries
4 cups Fresh Mixed Baby Greens
2 tablespoons Almonds, toasted and chopped

Directions:
1. Beat together all of the dressing ingredients in a bowl.
2. In another large serving bowl, mix together all of the salad ingredients. Combine the dressing with

the salad, tossing to coat well before serving immediately.

Apple, Pear & Celery Salad

This recipe is a perfect blend of fruits with fresh celery, spinach and a dressing. The cashew nut in this recipe adds a nice balance to the sweetness of the apple and pear.

MAKES: 2 servings
PREPARATION TIME: 15 minutes

For Dressing:
2 Scallions, chopped
½ Jalapeño Pepper, seeded and minced
1 teaspoon Fresh Ginger, minced
2 tablespoons Extra Virgin Olive Oil
2 tablespoons Balsamic Vinegar
1 tablespoon Pure Maple Syrup
Sea Salt, to taste

For Salad:
1 large Apple, peeled and spiralized
1 large Pear, peeled and spiralized or julienned
2 Celery Stalks, sliced thinly
2 cups Fresh Baby Spinach
2 tablespoons Basil Leaves, freshly chopped
¼ cup Cashew Nuts, roasted and chopped

Directions:
1. Beat together all of the dressing ingredients in a bowl.
2. In another large serving bowl, mix together all of

the salad ingredients, except for the cashew nuts. Combine the dressing with the salad and toss to coat well. Garnish with the cashew nuts and serve immediately.

Apple & Zucchini Salad

This is a truly delicious and nutritious salad with a satisfying crunch and fabulous vinaigrette. The raisins used in this dish complement the sweetness of the apple very nicely.

MAKES: 2 servings
PREPARATION TIME: 10 minutes

For Vinaigrette:
2 tablespoons Extra Virgin Olive Oil
1 tablespoon Apple Cider Vinegar
1 tablespoon Fresh Lemon juice
Sea Salt, to taste
Freshly Ground Black Pepper, to taste

For Salad:
1 large Apple, peeled and spiralized
1 medium Zucchini, spiralized
2 cups Romaine Lettuce, torn
¼ cup Raisins
2 tablespoons Pecans, chopped

Directions:
1. Beat together all of the vinaigrette ingredients in a bowl.
2. In another large serving bowl, mix together all of the salad ingredients, except for the pecans. Combine the dressing with the salad and toss to coat well. Garnish the salad with the pecans and

serve immediately.

Cucumber & Berry Salad

This is a refreshing salad which combines cucumbers, fresh mixed berries and a delicious sweet and sour dressing. This salad is ideal for any family gathering.

MAKES: 4 servings
PREPARATION TIME: 15 minutes

For Dressing:
1 tablespoon Sesame seeds
1 tablespoon Pure Maple Syrup
2 tablespoons Extra Virgin Olive Oil
2 tablespoons Apple Cider Vinegar
2 tablespoons Fresh Lemon juice
Sea Salt, to taste
Freshly Ground Black Pepper, to taste

For Salad:
2 large Cucumbers, spiralized
1 cup Fresh Blackberries
1 cup Fresh Raspberries
2 cups Fresh Strawberries, hulled and sliced
2 tablespoons Mint Leaves, freshly chopped

Directions:
1. Beat together all of the dressing ingredients in a bowl.
2. In another large serving bowl, mix together all of the salad ingredients, except for the mint. Combine

the dressing with the salad and toss to coat well. Garnish with the mint and serve immediately.

Cucumber & Cantaloupe Salad

This recipe makes an incredibly refreshing summer salad for the whole family. The avocado in this dish creates a wonderful creamy texture.

MAKES: 2 servings
PREPARATION TIME: 15 minutes

For Dressing:
1 tablespoon Extra Virgin Olive Oil
2 tablespoons Apple Cider Vinegar
2 teaspoons Fresh Lime juice
Sea Salt, to taste
Freshly Ground Black Pepper, to taste
1 tablespoon Mint Leaves, freshly minced

For Salad:
1 large Cucumber, spiralized
1 small Ripe Avocado, peeled, pitted and cubed
2 cups Cantaloupe, peeled, seeded and cubed

Directions:
1. Beat together all of the dressing ingredients in a bowl.
2. In another large serving bowl, mix together all of the salad ingredients. Combine the dressing with the salad and toss to coat well before serving immediately.

Cucumber & Greens Salad

This is a refreshingly delicious salad with a lovely crunchiness.
The vinaigrette brings a light heartiness to this salad.

MAKES: 2 servings
PREPARATION TIME: 15 minutes

For Vinaigrette:
1 tablespoon Fresh Oregano, minced
2 tablespoons Extra Virgin Olive Oil
1 tablespoon Balsamic Vinegar
1 tablespoon Fresh Lemon juice
Sea Salt, to taste
Freshly Ground Black Pepper, to taste

For Salad:
1 large Cucumber, spiralized
¼ cup Red Onion, spiralized or finely chopped
3 cups Fresh Mixed Greens

Directions:
1. Beat together all of the vinaigrette ingredients in a bowl.
2. In another large serving bowl, mix together all of the salad ingredients. Combine the vinaigrette with the salad and toss to coat well before serving immediately.

Cucumber & Scallion Salad

This salad has a wonderful crunchiness from the cucumbers and scallions, a crunchiness which is complemented nicely with the addition of creamy avocado. The dressing with this dish has a wonderful tangy flavor.

MAKES: 2 servings
PREPARATION TIME: 15 minutes

For Dressing:
1 Garlic Clove, minced
2 tablespoons minced Parsley Leaves
2 tablespoons Extra Virgin Olive Oil
1 tablespoon Balsamic Vinegar
1 tablespoon Fresh Lime juice
Sea Salt, to taste
Freshly Ground Black Pepper, to taste

For Salad:
2 large Cucumbers, spiralized
1 cup Scallions, chopped
½ cup Avocado, peeled, pitted and cubed

Directions:
1. Beat together all of the dressing ingredients in a bowl.
2. In another large serving bowl, mix together all of the salad ingredients. Combine the dressing with the salad and toss to coat well before serving

immediately.

Cucumber & Carrot Salad

This is a tasty and healthy salad. The peanut butter dressing adds a delicious creamy texture to this dish which may be loved by all.

MAKES: 4 servings
PREPARATION TIME: 15 minutes

For Dressing:
1 Garlic Clove, minced
½ teaspoon Fresh Ginger, minced
1 Jalapeño Pepper, seeded and minced
⅓ cup Peanut Butter
1 tablespoon Coconut Aminos
1 tablespoon Rice Vinegar
1 tablespoon Sesame Oil
1 tablespoon Brown Rice Syrup
Pinch of Red Pepper Flakes, crushed
¼ cup Warm Water

For Salad:
2 medium Cucumbers, spiralized
2 medium Carrots, spiralized
¼ cup Red Onion, chopped
4 cups Fresh Spinach Leaves, chopped

Directions:
1. Beat together all of the dressing ingredients in a bowl.
2. In another large serving bowl, mix together all of

the salad ingredients. Combine the dressing with the salad and toss to coat well before serving immediately.

Fennel & Celery Salad

This is an amazingly delicious and fresh salad recipe. The fresh cranberries give this salad a sweet tangy flavor with a beautiful color.

MAKES: 4 servings
PREPARATION TIME: 15 minutes

For Dressing:
1 tablespoon Mint Leaves, freshly chopped
2 tablespoons Extra Virgin Olive Oil
1 tablespoon Fresh Lime juice
Sea Salt, to taste
Freshly Ground Black Pepper, to taste

For Salad:
1 Fennel Bulb, spiralized
3 Celery Stalks, thinly sliced
1 Red Onion, spiralized
½ cup Fresh Cranberries
2 cups Baby Arugula
¼ cup Sesame Seeds

Directions:
1. Beat together all of the dressing ingredients in a bowl.
2. In another large serving bowl, mix together all of the salad ingredients, except for the sesame seeds. Combine the dressing with the salad and toss to

coat well. Garnish with the sesame seeds and serve immediately.

Zucchini & Mixed Vegetable Salad

This is a filling and light salad with a salty, tangy and crunchy texture. The dressing with this salad perfectly balances the flavors.

MAKES: 4 servings
PREPARATION TIME: 20 minutes

For Dressing:
2 tablespoons Extra Virgin Olive Oil
2 tablespoons Fresh Lime juice
2 tablespoons Balsamic Vinegar
¼ teaspoon Dried Basil, crushed
¼ teaspoon Dried Oregano, crushed
¼ teaspoon Dried Thyme, crushed
Pinch of Red Pepper Flakes, crushed
Sea Salt, to taste
Freshly Ground Black Pepper, to taste

For Salad:
2 large Zucchinis, spiralized
1 cup Cherry Tomatoes, halved
1 cup Artichoke Hearts, quartered
½ cup Black Olives, pitted and sliced
1 Red Onion, chopped

Directions:
1. Beat together all of the dressing ingredients in a bowl.
2. In another large serving bowl, mix together all of

the salad ingredients. Combine the dressing with the salad and toss to coat well before serving immediately.

Zucchini & Avocado Salad

This recipe makes a quick and delicious salad with zucchini and avocado. Enjoy this dish as a great choice to accompany summer meals or otherwise.

MAKES: 2 servings
PREPARATION TIME: 10 minutes

1 large Zucchini, spiralized
1 medium Avocado, peeled, pitted and cubed
1 tablespoon Chives, minced
1 Tablespoon Fresh Cilantro Leaves, minced
1 tablespoon Extra Virgin Olive Oil
1 tablespoon Fresh Lime Juice
Pinch of Red Pepper Flakes, crushed
Sea Salt and Freshly Ground Black Pepper, to taste

Directions:

1. In a large serving bowl, add all ingredients and toss to coat well.
2. Serve immediately.

Zucchini, Carrot & Cucumber Salad

*This is a tasty, refreshingly crunchy and a flavorful salad.
Additionally, this salad is finished with a delicious slightly sweet
and tangy creamy dressing.*

MAKES: 2 servings
PREPARATION TIME: 15 minutes

For Dressing:
*¼ cup Soy-Free Veganaise
1 tablespoon Fresh Lime juice
1 teaspoon Extra Virgin Olive Oil
2 tablespoons Pure Maple Syrup
1 teaspoon Dried Dill, crushed
Sea Salt, to taste
Freshly Ground Black Pepper, to taste*

For Salad:
*1 medium Zucchini, spiralized
1 small Cucumber, spiralized
1 small Carrot, peeled and spiralized*

Directions:
1. Beat together all of the dressing ingredients in a bowl.
2. In another large serving bowl, mix together all of the salad ingredients. Combine the dressing with the salad and toss to coat well before serving immediately.

Zucchini & Bell Pepper Salad

This is a simple, light and filling salad. It may be a great hit to accompany any springtime gathering.

MAKES: 2 servings
PREPARATION TIME: 20 minutes

For Dressing:
1 Garlic Clove, minced
1 tablespoon minced Cilantro Leaves
2 tablespoons Extra Virgin Olive Oil
2 tablespoons Fresh Lime juice
Pinch of Red Pepper Flakes, crushed
Sea Salt, to taste
Freshly Ground Black Pepper, to taste

For Salad:
1 small Zucchini, spiralized
1 Broccoli Stem, spiralized or thinly sliced
½ small Red Bell Pepper, seeded and thinly sliced
½ small Yellow Bell Pepper, seeded and thinly sliced
½ small Orange Bell Pepper, seeded and thinly sliced

Directions:
1. Beat together all of the dressing ingredients in a bowl.
2. In another large serving bowl, mix together all of the salad ingredients. Combine the dressing with the salad and toss to coat well before serving immediately.

⑥

IT'S WORTH IT

Many persons would agree that spiralizing can be addictive. Well, positively so. But the good news is that the overall health benefits of creating tasty spiralized vegan recipes are amazing. Moreover, preparing inspiring vegan meals with the spiralizer is a welcome idea to many vegan home cooks. With this book, you'll be always equipped to make a reasonable variety of vegan meals.

Like me, you may have started out with the standard way of eating a combination of animal-based foods, plant-based foods and everything in-between. However, if you really want to experience natural healing and optimum health, then the vegan lifestyle is the way to go. The vegan lifestyle is well rated for promoting weight loss, preventing and reversing heart disease, reducing the risk of Alzheimer's disease, preventing or curing diabetes, lowering blood pressure and increasing overall longevity. Hence, for the most part, eating vegan doesn't only treat a lot of chronic diseases, but it actually reverses them. Furthermore, you can even unclog blocked arteries by following a vegan diet, and that in itself is simply amazing. Isn't it?

All in all, thank you for choosing my vegan spiralizer cookbook. I would appreciate it, if you would let other readers know about your experience. Let's stay vegan inspired!

Cheers to good health,
Beth Solomon

CONVERSION CHART

If you are living in the UK, you may use this measurement conversion chart to easily convert any of these recipes. You may find the following very convenient if you are uncertain of any particular measurement or conversion.

FOR LIQUID INGREDIENTS

1 teaspoon (tsp) = **6 milliliters (ml)**
1 tablespoon (tbsp) = **15 milliliters (ml)**
1/8 cup = **30 milliliters (ml)**
¼ cup = **60 milliliters (ml)**
½ cup = **120 milliliters (ml)**
1 cup = **240 milliliters (ml)**

FOR DRY OR SOLID INGREDIENTS

1 teaspoon (tsp) = **5 grams (g)**
1 tablespoon (tbsp) = **15 grams (g)**
1 ounce (oz) = **28 grams (g)**

1 cup flour = **150 grams (g)**
1 cup sugar = **175 grams (g)**
1 cup spiralized fruit or vegetable = **175 grams (g)**
1 small spiralized fruit or other vegetable = **120 - 150 grams (g)**
1 medium spiralized fruit or vegetable = **195 -225 grams (g)**
1 large spiralized fruit or vegetable = **250 -315 grams (g)**
1 cup nuts or seeds = **200 grams (g)**
1/8 cup nut butter = **30 grams (g)**
¼ cup nut butter = **55 grams (g)**
1/3 cup nut butter = **75 grams (g)**
½ cup nut butter = **115 grams (g)**
2/3 cup nut butter = **150 grams (g)**
¾ cup nut butter = **170 grams (g)**
1 cup nut butter = **225 grams (g)**

OVEN TEMPERATURES

275° Fahrenheit (F) = **140° Celsius (C)** or Gas Mark 1
300° Fahrenheit (F) = **150° Celsius (C)** or Gas Mark 2
325° Fahrenheit (F) = **165° Celsius (C)** or Gas Mark 3

350° Fahrenheit (F) = **180° Celsius (C)** or Gas Mark 4
375° Fahrenheit (F) = **190° Celsius (C)** or Gas Mark 5
400° Fahrenheit (F) = **200° Celsius (C)** or Gas Mark 6
425° Fahrenheit (F) = **220° Celsius (C)** or Gas Mark 7
450° Fahrenheit (F) = **230° Celsius (C)** or Gas Mark 8

Printed in Germany
by Amazon Distribution
GmbH, Leipzig